Adventures in the
# GREAT OUTDOORS

# CAMPING

Robyn
Hardyman

Raintree is an imprint of Capstone Global Library Limited, a company incorporated in England and Wales having its registered office at 264 Banbury Road, Oxford, OX2 7DY – Registered company number: 6695582

**www.raintree.co.uk**
myorders@raintree.co.uk

Text © Capstone Global Library Limited 2016
The moral rights of the proprietor have been asserted.

Produced for Raintree by Calcium
Edited by Sarah Eason and Katie Woolley
Designed by Emma DeBanks
Picture research by Sarah Eason
Production by Victoria Fitzgerald
Originated by Capstone Global Library Ltd © 2016
Printed and bound in China

ISBN 978 1 4747 1547 8 (hardback)
19 18 17 16 15
10 9 8 7 6 5 4 3 2 1

ISBN 978 1 4747 1550 8 (paperback)
20 19 18 17 16
10 9 8 7 6 5 4 3 2 1

**British Library Cataloguing in Publication Data**
A full catalogue record for this book is available from the British Library.

**Acknowledgements**
We would like to thank the following for permission to reproduce photographs: Dreamstime: Alyssand 29, Baldas1950 27, Crazygood40 9t, 9m, Fireflyphoto 24, Hallgerd 13, Jeffbanke 17, Katseyephoto 20, Mathayward 14, Mikdam 26, Monkeybusinessimages 18, Paulmaguire 16t, Photosky 8, Russelllinton 19, Stargatechris 9b, Sutsaiy 22, Tbroucek 15, Zestmarina 21; Shutterstock: Lisa A 11, Claude Beaubien 7, Brocreative 6b, Cheryl Casey 10, Gorillaimages 28, Morgan Lane Photography 1, 5, 16b, 23, 25, Varina and Jay Patel 12, Pavzyuk Svitlana 4, Wong Sze Yuen 6t.

Cover photographs reproduced with permission of: Shutterstock: Kokhanchikov.

Some words are shown in bold, **like this**. You can find out what they mean by looking in the glossary.

# CONTENTS

# GO WILD!

It is time to go outside for a real adventure! When you leave the world of home, television, computers and school behind, you enter the amazing world of nature. You are can explore, play and go wild!

Going on a camping trip is the perfect way to get in touch with the natural world and discover its wonders up close. You will be sleeping under the stars, surrounded by the woods, or out on the beach with the sounds of the sea in your ears. Maybe you will be in the mountains, with a huge **landscape** of nature laid out before you. How amazing is that?

*You will have an incredible view if you camp on the beach.*

A camping trip is a great way to make friends.

Camping gives you the chance to spend some time with your friends and family. You can play together, explore together and cook and talk together. You will learn new skills, too, such as **pitching** a **tent**, making a fire or finding your way on a **hike**. Maybe you will learn something about yourself, too. You might even find out that you are braver than you thought!

For a successful camping trip, you need to plan ahead, and think about where you want to go and what you will need. You also need to behave properly while you are in the wild. Let your imagination run free, but always look after your **environment** and remember that it can be dangerous, too. That way, you will make sure you have a wonderful adventure!

5

# PLAN YOUR TRIP

You will enjoy your camping trip far more if you have planned it well before you go. There is a lot to think about. What kind of **location** are you looking for? How long do you want to be away? What will the weather be like? Spend some time on these questions so you can find the perfect place to camp and plan what you need to take there.

The world is a big place! Are you going to a beach, some woods or mountains? Will you be travelling far and staying long? You are most likely to be camping for just a few days in a location close to home. Do some research at home to find the perfect places for your trip. With an adult, look in books and on the internet for great locations near you.

*Researching locations together helps to get everyone in the mood for camping!*

*Hillside locations are quiet and peaceful places for camping.*

*Camping on large campsites with many other people can be noisy, but fun, too!*

**STAY SAFE!**
Make sure the location you choose is free from **hazards** such as flooding or tall cliffs.

You can choose between a campsite and the open countryside. If you choose to go to a campsite, find out which sites are best and whether you need to make a reservation. Some campsites do not allow fires, so if you are dreaming of marshmallows and songs around a campfire at night, choose carefully! If you choose a wild location, make sure you find out whether camping is permitted.

# GET THE GEAR

Having the right gear can make all the difference to the success of a camping trip. When it comes to camping equipment and **gadgets**, there is so much to choose! It is a good idea to get expert advice in a camping shop. The most important items to choose are the right tent and a good **sleeping bag**.

Choose your tent carefully. Tents range from **lightweight**, single-person models, to large tents in which a whole family can sleep. Some tents can cope with extreme weather, while others are designed for more gentle use. Sleeping bags are rated by their warmth. If you are going up a mountain, choose a warm one! To sleep comfortably, you will need a **sleeping mat**, too.

*A dome tent (pictured) is a good choice for two or three people, while a cabin-style tent gives you room to stand up.*

STAY SAFE!

Do not forget to pack a first aid kit for emergencies and a torch for seeing in the dark.

*Choose comfortable footwear to keep your feet dry and warm. Hiking boots are perfect if you are going on a hike.*

Clothes are particularly important for comfort and warmth when you are camping. Having several thin layers is best, so you can add more or take some off to suit the **temperature**. Keep your legs covered to protect yourself from scrapes and insects, and wear comfortable shoes so you can easily get around. If you are going to be hiking, consider taking hiking shoes or boots, and a waterproof coat.

If you are not making a real fire you will need a stove for cooking, such as a portable gas stove. Take basic pans, plates and utensils and something to wash dishes in. A large container is useful for carrying water. Do not forget to plan what you are going to eat, and pack all the ingredients. Remember to bring matches!

*A sleeping mat makes sleeping on the ground much more comfortable.*

# WE HAVE ARRIVED!

**You have found the perfect location. It may be on a fabulous beach, beside a lake or deep in the woods. Wherever you are, make sure you choose a really great place to set up camp.**

There are a few things to remember when picking your camping spot, whatever the type of landscape you are in. Firstly, choose level ground.

Next, you will need a source of clean, flowing water nearby for drinking and washing. This is easy to find on a campsite. It can be more difficult in open countryside because you will need to find a river or stream. Do not camp too close to water, though, or you might be at risk of flooding. Finally, you need a cooking area for your camp. This should be near the tents, but not too close, for fire safety.

**STAY SAFE!**

On the beach, make sure you set up camp away from the incoming tide.

*Tents can be put up quite quickly, but make sure you practise beforehand.*

# COLLECTING RAINWATER

You can drink pure rainwater while camping. Here is how!

1 Position your table in an open area, away from any overhanging bushes or trees.

2 Put the container on the table.

3 After it has rained, collect the container and empty any rainwater into a clean flask.

4 Always boil your rainwater or add a water purification tablet to it before drinking it.

5 Enjoy your fresh, clean rainwater!

**You will need:**
- large, clean container
- water purification tablets
- clean flask
- camping table

*Pure rainwater tastes great if treated properly.*

# STAY CLEAN

**Half the fun of living outdoors and having an adventure in the wild is getting dirty. It is all part of camping! However, it is still important to be able to clean yourself and your gear at the end of the day.**

At a campsite, water for washing and cooking is provided by a tap. You will need strong containers for carrying drinking water from the water source to your tent. In open countryside, you will have pitched camp close to a flowing water source such as a stream or river. **Stagnant** water, such as that in a pond, is not safe to drink or to wash with. If you drink stagnant water, or swallow it while washing, it can make you very ill. Always use a stream to wash the dishes or collect water for cooking and drinking.

In the great outdoors it is fine to get a bit dirty!

It is especially important to wash yourself after a busy day exploring. It is easy to pick up **germs** when you are getting close to nature. Watch out, though, because the river water may feel very cold! Always wash your hands before you handle food or eat. If you are camping for more than a few days, you may need to wash some of your clothes, too. Hang them up to dry in the sun and wind.

You do not want to **pollute** a natural water source with chemicals, so try to use as little soap as possible. Make sure you wash yourself and brush your teeth downstream from where you collect drinking water. That way you will not be drinking soapy water.

*A morning wash in a cold stream will wake you up and get you ready for the day!*

STAY SAFE!
Streams and rivers can be fast flowing. Never get in the water to wash.

# READY FOR FUN

**The camp is all set up, and it is time for some fun! There are many great ways to have a good time outdoors, so get in touch with your wild side.**

The beach, fields and woods are full of great places to play. With sticks, mud, sand, stones or leaves, you can make any number of tools and games. If you have prepared really well for your trip, you might even find you have a few extra items from home that can help to make great tools. Try making a **catapult** from a Y-shaped stick and a thick rubber band. Tie the rubber band tightly around each arm of the stick. Or make a **blowpipe** by hollowing out the soft stem from a tree. Sharpen the end of a harder stick and use it to get the soft insides out of the stem.

STAY SAFE!

Ask an adult to help you sharpen any sticks.

*Explore your environment and discover an amazing natural playground.*

Big groups can play some great games. Try "Capture the flag". This is a game in which two teams each have a **territory**. You can mark the territory with some stones or branches, and you can use coloured chalk to put the colour of each team on the markers used. Each team must battle to take a "flag" from their **opponents**' territory, while still trying to **defend** their own territory!

You could even try setting up a treasure hunt, with a lot of clues around camp. Try hiding items such as stones or sticks that you have marked with messages or clues about where the next find might be. Then ask your friends to find the treasure!

# NATURE WATCH

**Camping is one of the best ways to get close to nature, and the great outdoors is full of fantastic places to explore and animals to see.**

If you are camping in the woods, look up in the trees to see all the birds and animals living around you. On the ground, piles of leaves and rotting logs make great homes for insects. Use a magnifying glass to look at them up-close. If you are near a river or lake, lie flat on the ground near the water. See what is swimming in the depths, or skimming the surface.

You can see different things at different times of day. Many creatures prefer to come out in the early morning or evening. Look for different animal tracks and different types of animal waste, too.

Deer can be found by looking for the tracks they leave.

A walk in the woods is a great way to hunt for insects.

# TRACKING ANIMALS

Animals are all around you outdoors. You can find them by following the tracks they leave behind.

1 Look all around you for any signs of tracks. Search in the mud or leaves, or look for broken twigs on bushes and trees.

2 If you see a track mark, try to identify it using your guidebook.

3 Follow the tracks to see where they go, then use your binoculars and try to spot the animal.

EXPLORE THIS!

**You will need:**

- animal track guidebook
- binoculars

Look for animal tracks in wet soil or sand.

Deer tracks

STAY SAFE!

Always make sure you have an adult with you while tracking animals.

17

# HIKING AND FISHING

While you are out in the wild, why not explore even further by going for a hike? Hiking is a great way to see the countryside up-close, and it is great exercise, too. If you prefer, you could go fishing and catch your own dinner! There is always a lot of wildlife around wild, watery places, so while you are fishing, look out for animals and plants around you.

To make the most of your hike, put on your hiking boots, pack some water and a map in a small rucksack and head off into the wild! You can see so much more when you are on the move. Listen for the birds, and look carefully all around you to see nature in action. Do not forget to take an animal identification guidebook and camera with you. That way you will be able to work out which animals you have seen and take photos of them.

**STAY SAFE!** Always go hiking with an adult and stay on marked paths.

*See nature up-close on a hike.*

If you are camping near water, why not try out fishing? You will need some basic equipment, such as a **fishing rod** and line, some **bait**, a hook, a float and a net. With an adult, check that fishing is permitted, then find a good place to fish. This may be shady water beneath trees or a still pool. Cast your line into the water and wait. You will be amazed at all the wildlife you see as you sit still. Release your catch back into the water or cook it for dinner!

# THE CAMPFIRE

**A great campfire is the heart of camp. Everyone loves the smell of wood smoke, the crackle of logs and the flickering flames. You can gather around your campfire to eat, sing or tell stories.**

To make your campfire, start by clearing the area of all **debris**. Make a ring of rocks to surround your fire. You need three types of material to burn. Firstly, find tiny twigs, dry grass, bark or wood shavings, to light the fire. Secondly, you need small, dry sticks, called **kindling**. These will burn easily. Finally, collect larger sticks and logs to burn for a longer time. Collect all three types, and stack them in piles away from the fire site.

*This type of fire pit takes a while to make, but it will burn for a long time. You can also use it more than once.*

Make a loose pile of the dry twigs and grass in the middle of the ring. With your back to the wind, strike a match and light the pile. Put the match in the pile, too. You may need to blow on it gently to get it going. Once it is burning, add small pieces of kindling. The wood can be either stacked up in a pyramid shape, or criss-crossed in a pile. Either way, make sure that air can always get into the base. When the fire is really going well, add the larger logs, one at a time. Put more large logs around the fire for everyone to sit on.

Let the fire burn down to ash, and then put it out completely. Scatter the ashes and sprinkle with water. Drench any charred logs.

*A carefully-made fire can burn for several hours.*

**STAY SAFE!**

Never make a fire under trees or in windy conditions. It could easily spread out of control.

# MAKE A FEAST

**It is evening and everyone is hungry. It is time for food! Campsite food is best kept simple so it is easy to make on camping cooking equipment.**

You will have decided at home how you are going to cook your food. It may be a grill over an open fire, a pan over a gas stove or simply some wooden skewers to hold over the campfire flames. You can cook most fish, meat and vegetables with this simple equipment. Make sure that your food and equipment have been thoroughly washed before you begin to cook.

STAY SAFE!

Always ask an adult to handle the hot food and pans.

*Food tastes especially good when it is cooked and eaten outdoors.*

# CAMPFIRE COOK

Marshmallows toasted on an open fire make the best camping snack ever.

1 Once your campfire is lit, carefully push a marshmallow onto the end of a long stick.

2 Hold the marshmallow near the fire or just above the flames.

3 Toast the marshmallow for a few seconds until it is warm, gooey and ready to eat!

**EXPLORE THIS!**

**You will need:**
- campfire
- marshmallows
- long sticks for toasting

*Toast gooey marshmallows as evening falls.*

23

# FUN AFTER DARK

**As evening comes and you are feeling a little sleepy, sit around the campfire. Make the most of having no televisions and no computers. Telling stories around the campfire and singing songs are great ways to have fun instead.**

The countryside gets wilder at night, too, when different animals come out. You may not be able to see them, but there are other ways of knowing they are there. Listen out for the call of owls in the darkness or the rustle of rabbits, deer and mice in the bushes.

A lot of insects come out at night, too. In the evening, you will find that some amazing insects are attracted by your camp lights. In some areas you might see fireflies, too. These creatures are actually beetles with wings, and they produce flashes of light at night that light up the darkness around you.

*Fireflies give off a glowing light at night.*

24

*Try making scary shadows against your tent walls to really scare each other!*

As the last light fades, you can try making up spooky stories to thrill and chill you in the dark! One person starts the story off with a scary sentence. The next person adds another sentence. Scared yet? Continue around the campfire two or three times to finish the story. Or how about a "truth or dare" session? Each person has to tell a secret about themselves or accept a dare.

If things get too spooky, change the mood with some campfire singing. Make your songs silly and fun until everyone is laughing. Songs like "Ging gang goolie" can go on for hours and hours!

25

# STARRY NIGHT

**Sleeping out under the stars is amazing. There is nothing above you but the enormous sky and the stars twinkling far away, deep in space.**

It is completely dark, you are out in the countryside and you are **connected** with nature like never before. The sounds and smells of the outdoors are more intense than ever. Can you see the moon hanging in the sky, casting silvery shadows over everything around you?

While camping in the wild, there are no street lights or pollution fumes to lighten the night sky. This makes it a great time for stargazing.

*Enjoy the peace of the night after all your adventures in the wild.*

# STARGAZING

Gazing up at the stars is the perfect way to end a day's camping.

**You will need:**
- huge, clear sky full of stars
- binoculars
- guidebook on the constellations

1 Lie down in your sleeping bags, with heads close together and bodies fanned out in a circle, like the spokes of a bicycle wheel.

2 Turn off any lights you have shining in the camp. They make it harder to see the stars.

3 Once your eyes have become used to the dark, try to find patterns in the stars.

4 Take turns to look through the binoculars. You will see thousands of stars!

5 One person can look up a few **constellations**, or star groups, in the guidebook and point them out to the others.

6 If you are really lucky, you may see a shooting star.

*Look up into the night sky. What can you see?*

# GO GREEN

**We all have a responsibility to keep the countryside safe and unspoilt for the future. That way, everyone can continue to enjoy it. Whatever your outdoor adventure, remember to respect the natural world and make as little impact on it as you can.**

Leaving litter, camping equipment or food behind can spoil a beautiful, natural space and harm the wildlife that live there. Remember, whatever you take with you on your camping trip needs to be taken back home again!

Having a great camping adventure is all about looking, discovering and enjoying, but not disturbing your location. There are several things to think about when you try to leave no trace behind. While you are having fun in the woods, for example, do not carve on tree trunks. Never write graffiti anywhere, though writing your name in the sand on the beach, to be washed away by the sea, is just fine!

*Make sure you pack up all your equipment and take it home.*

*Leave the landscape as beautiful as you found it so that others can come and enjoy it, too.*

Leave behind the plants and flowers you discover so that others can enjoy them, too. And it is never a good idea to chase, feed or try to touch any animals you come across, even if they are really tiny! Wild animals are meant to be wild, so never treat them like a pet.

When it is time to **strike** your camp, make sure you take your gear home with you, including any litter. The idea is to leave your location as clean as you found it. Or, if it was not very clean, clean it up for future adventurers. If you leave no trace behind you, no one else will ever know you were there!

# GLOSSARY

**bait** food that is put on a hook to catch fish

**blowpipe** tube for shooting out pellets by blowing

**catapult** device used for shooting objects

**connected** linked to or having to do with

**constellation** group of stars

**debris** loose bits and pieces such as rocks and twigs

**defend** protect

**environment** all the living things and conditions of a place

**fishing rod** long pole with a line attached for fishing

**gadget** piece of mechanical or electronic equipment

**germ** tiny organism that can cause disease

**hazard** danger or risk, such as flooding or steep cliffs

**hike** long walk

**kindling** small pieces of wood used to start a fire

**landscape** large, wild area

**lightweight** not heavy

**location** place, such as a campsite or field

**opponent** person who is against you

**pitching** putting up a tent

**pollute** make dirty, or to harm by adding chemicals

**sleeping bag** padded bag to sleep in while camping

**sleeping mat** thin, soft mat to sleep on

**stagnant** water that does not flow, but is still

**strike** to take down and pack up your camping equipment

**temperature** how hot or cold something is

**tent** shelter that can be put up and taken down easily

**territory** area a person or animal considers to be their own or belonging to them

# FIND OUT MORE

## Books

*2015 Guide to the Night Sky*, S. Dunlop and W. Tirion
  (Collins, 2014)

*Camping and Hiking (Get Outdoors)*, Neil Champion
  (Wayland, 2014)

*Camping (Mission: Explore)*, The Geography Collective
  (Can of Worms Kids Press, 2011)

*Minibeasts (Outdoor Explorers)*, Sandy Green
  (Franklin Watts, 2013)

## Websites

**astronomynow.com/uk-sky-chart**
Identify star constellations visible on your camping trip. Choose
the correct year, month and time from the drop-down menus,
print your star chart and take it with you on your expedition.

**www.naturedetectives.org.uk/download/hunt_
minibeasts.htm**
Print these minibeast identification lists before your camping trip.

**www.scouthelp.co.uk/Countryside_Code**
Learn all about the Countryside Code and help to protect the
natural world while you are camping or hiking.

# INDEX